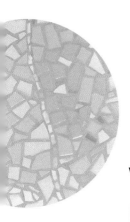

Contents

What are mosaics?

A mosaic is a special kind of artwork. It is made up of small coloured pieces, arranged side by side to create a picture or pattern. The pieces are most often coloured stones or glass. When they are stuck down or set in cement, the picture becomes a very solid object. Some examples in this book have survived all sorts of upheavals – even volcanic eruptions – for 2,000 years.

The toughness of mosaics gives them important advantages. They can be put up outdoors, in exposed public places. They also make remarkably hard-wearing floor surfaces. Literally millions of visitors to the National Gallery in London have walked on the fifty-year-old Defiance mosaic on page 18! Inside buildings, mosaics make striking wall and ceiling decorations.

▲ *The dome of the Sheikh Lotfallah Mosque in Isfahan, Iran. Dating from the early 16th century is covered with superb mosaics.*

Past and present

Mosaics have a long history. 5,000 years ago, people in the Middle East were creating patterns on walls by pressing pieces of clay into them. Later, artists in Islamic societies put up dazzling mosaic domes and filled other surfaces with **abstract** or flower patterns. Across the Atlantic, the Aztecs of Mexico and other peoples covered objects such as figures and masks with mosaics of turquoise and other semi-precious stones.

The ancient Greeks founded a different tradition. They made mosaics that were pictures of people and animals, often shown in scenes that were part of a story. Then the Romans took up mosaic-making and spread it all over their vast empire. Many Greek and Roman mosaics have scenes from the stories they most enjoyed, such as **myths** and legends about gods and heroes and long-ago wars. For centuries after the Roman Empire was converted to Christianity, mosaics were used lavishly in churches to tell biblical stories.

In recent times, mosaics have often been chosen for large-scale decorations on public buildings. Look at the floors and walls of town halls, museums and libraries – you will be surprised by how often you see a mosaic you hadn't noticed before. Nowadays, mosaic artists work in all sorts of styles, often to decorate houses or gardens. The ancient art of mosaic is as popular as ever.

▲ *This two-headed serpent, covered with turquoise and shell mosaic, was made around 1400–1520 by a craftsman in Aztec Mexico.*

How to use this book

Background information on each mosaic featured, including its designer, date, location and history

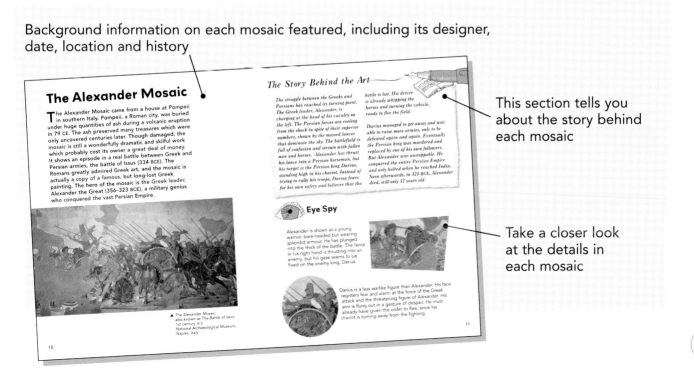

This section tells you about the story behind each mosaic

Take a closer look at the details in each mosaic

How are mosaics made?

The ancient Greeks pioneered a basic form of mosaic. Around 800 BCE, they started arranging pebbles of different colours into pictures. Later, they painted some of the pebbles to brighten the **composition**, achieving strikingly bold results. Pebble mosaics are still often used, especially for outdoor settings such as gardens.

▲ This pebble mosaic from Pella in Greece dates from the 4th century BCE. The stones have not been worked on, but keep their natural shapes. The design, although ancient, looks like something from a modern garden!

The Greeks and Romans soon found that, if they wanted more detailed mosaic pictures, they had to use smaller stones that fitted closely together. So mosaic makers cut the stones into little cubes or other shapes needed to follow the outlines in the picture. These small pieces were known by the Latin name *tesserae*. A cement and sand mixture, called **grout**, stuck the sides together. Rubbed down and polished, the flat surfaces of the tesserae created a pleasing and practical floor decoration.

Mosaics were too heavy to use on walls and ceilings until the 1st century BCE when a lightweight glass was introduced and replaced stones for many purposes. The glass was coloured, or was made to look golden by putting gold foil inside it. Set at angles to catch the light, the gilded backgrounds of church mosaics created dazzling effects.

Working methods

Mosaic artists have used two main working methods. The **direct method** is to draw the design on to the plaster or other **adhesive** backing. Then the bases of the stones are set directly into place. The **indirect** or **reverse method** is slower, but gives the artist greater control. It involves using a full-scale guide drawing, called a **cartoon**. The drawing is done as a reverse or mirror image of the final work. Following the design, the tesserae are lightly pasted, face down, on to the cartoon. It may then be cut into sections. Each section is turned upside down on to a board. From these the assembled tesserae are slid into their permanent cement base. When the cartoon and paste are washed off, the image is seen the right way round.

▲ *This wall mosaic was designed by Shug Jones and Lynne Chinn in 2005. Called 'Tracks of Our Past and Future', it is 23m long and celebrates the African-American Douglass Community of Plano, Texas, USA.*

Modern mosaic artists try to achieve all sorts of effects. They may work with unusual materials such as shells, crockery or mother of pearl, or they may use manufactured glass and other commercial products.

The tools used to create mosaics, though now made by machines, have hardly changed over the centuries. Only a few jobs, such as rubbing down and polishing, are no longer done by hand. The talent and skill of the mosaic artist remain as important as ever.

The Alexander Mosaic

The Alexander Mosaic came from a house at Pompeii in southern Italy. Pompeii, a Roman city, was buried under huge quantities of ash during a volcanic eruption in 79 CE. The ash preserved many treasures which were only uncovered centuries later. Though damaged, the mosaic is still a wonderfully dramatic and skilful work which probably cost its owner a great deal of money. It shows an episode in a real battle between Greek and Persian armies, the battle of Issus (334 BCE). The Romans greatly admired Greek art, and the mosaic is actually a copy of a famous, but long-lost Greek painting. The hero of the mosaic is the Greek leader, Alexander the Great (356–323 BCE), a military genius who conquered the vast Persian Empire.

▲ *The Alexander Mosaic*
also known as The Battle of Issus
1st century BCE
National Archaeological Museum,
Naples, Italy

The Story Behind the Art

The struggle between the Greeks and Persians has reached its turning point. The Greek leader, Alexander, is charging at the head of his cavalry on the left. The Persian forces are reeling from the shock in spite of their superior numbers, shown by the massed lances that dominate the sky. The battlefield is full of confusion and strewn with fallen men and horses. Alexander has thrust his lance into a Persian horseman, but his target is the Persian king Darius, standing high in his chariot. Instead of trying to rally his troops, Darius fears for his own safety and believes that the battle is lost. His driver is already whipping the horses and turning the vehicle, ready to flee the field.

Darius managed to get away and was able to raise more armies, only to be defeated again and again. Eventually the Persian king was murdered and replaced by one of his own followers. But Alexander was unstoppable. He conquered the entire Persian Empire and only halted when he reached India. Soon afterwards, in 323 BCE, Alexander died, still only 32 years old.

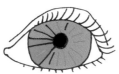 **Eye Spy**

Alexander is shown as a young warrior, bare-headed but wearing splendid armour. He has plunged into the thick of the battle. The lance in his right hand is thrusting into an enemy, but his gaze seems to be fixed on the enemy king, Darius.

Darius is a less warlike figure than Alexander. His face registers fear and alarm at the force of the Greek attack and the threatening figure of Alexander. His arm is flung out in a gesture of despair. He must already have given the order to flee, since his chariot is turning away from the fighting.

The Judgement of Paris

The Judgement of Paris was originally part of a large and beautiful mosaic floor in Antioch, a city in Syria that belonged to the Roman Empire. The story is one of the many Greek myths and legends that the Romans also enjoyed. Most of the characters in these stories can be called by their Greek or their Roman names. For example, the Greek goddesses Athene, Hera and Aphrodite are also known by the Roman names Athena, Minerva and Venus. The story behind the Judgement of Paris belongs to a large group of linked tales about how the legendary Trojan War broke out and what happened during and after it.

◄ The Judgement of Paris
2nd century CE
Louvre Museum, Paris, France

The Story Behind the Art

The young shepherd Paris is faced with a difficult decision. He must judge which of three goddesses is the most beautiful. In the picture, Paris is seated, thinking. Beside him is the messenger of the gods, Hermes, who has given Paris his task. The goddesses are placed in front of the young man and are trying to influence his choice. Warlike Athene (far left) offers him military glory if he chooses her. In the centre, Hera, wife of the king of the gods, sits on a throne. She tells Paris that if he chooses her, he will rule Asia. Aphrodite, goddess of love, stands at the right, in a lovely blue gown. Her offer is the love of the most beautiful woman in the world. Faced with a choice between fame, power and love, Paris decides that love is what he wants. He chooses Aphrodite.

Afterwards, all goes well for Paris for a time. He is recognised as a long-lost son of the king of Troy. He becomes a prince and is sent on a mission to the Greek city of Sparta. There he meets Sparta's beautiful queen, Helen, who is married to King Menelaus. As Aphrodite promised, Helen falls in love with Paris and runs away with him to Troy.

Then the romance turns into tragedy. The Greeks, feeling insulted, assemble an army to recover Helen and take revenge on Paris. They sail for Troy and besiege it for ten years. Many men die during the war, and at its end the city of Troy is a smoking ruin.

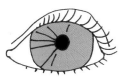

Eye Spy

The winged sandals identify Hermes (Roman name Mercury) as the swift messenger of the gods. He also carries a special staff, the **caduceus**, with a serpent wrapped round it.

A little goat drinks from a pool. The blue glass of the pool creates the shimmering look of water.

Eros (Roman name Cupid) is the child of Aphrodite. His presence signals her victory in the contest.

Defiance

The National Gallery in London has Britain's largest national collection of paintings. But the first works of art on show are marble mosaics at the main entrance. Many people don't notice them because the entrance is usually crowded and the mosaics are on the floor under their feet! The mosaics celebrate Britain and the British way of life. They are all by the Russian-born artist Boris Anrep (1883–1969), a mosaic specialist who designed and made the works in his Paris **studio**. Defiance belongs to a group of mosaics that Anrep called 'The Modern Virtues'. It was directly inspired by Britain's part in the Second World War.

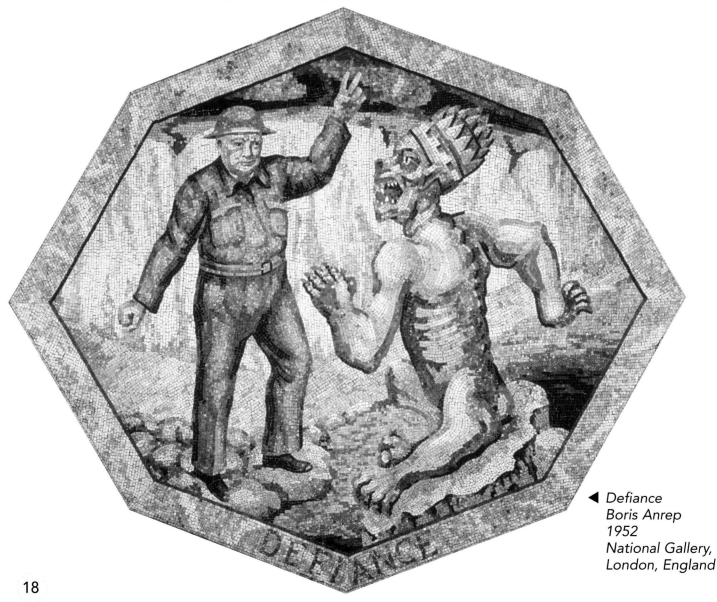

◀ *Defiance*
Boris Anrep
1952
National Gallery,
London, England

The Story Behind the Art

Defiance records a historic moment in the early part of the Second World War (1939–45). In 1940, Germany defeated France and Britain. France was forced to surrender, and Britain was left to face a mighty enemy who ruled most of Europe. Britain's prime minister, Winston Churchill, declared that Britain would fight on, and he expressed the nation's determination in a series of great speeches.

Anrep's mosaic shows Churchill standing in front of the white cliffs of Dover, symbolising Britain. He wears his most famous wartime outfit – a helmet and overalls (very unusual at a time when upper-class people normally wore suits

in public). He raises his left hand, making a V-for-Victory sign; his right hand is clenched in a fist. The other figure, dominating a conquered Europe, stands for Nazi Germany and its leader, Adolf Hitler. It is shown as a monster, dancing with rage at Churchill's refusal to submit.

During this period, British fighter planes defeated the Germans in the air during the **Battle of Britain***. Britain also withstood heavy bombing (* **the Blitz** *). Then in 1941, Russia and the USA were drawn into the war on Britain's side. The strength of the two sides changed dramatically, dooming Germany and its allies.*

 **Eye Spy**

Coming to power when defeat seemed likely, Churchill often made this encouraging V-for-Victory sign.

The monster is in the shape of the swastika symbol used by the Nazis on flags, uniforms and **insignia**. The creature's frenzy also suggests the famous rages of the Nazi leader, Adolf Hitler.

The monster stands for Nazi Germany. It is also like the Beast described in biblical prophecies, crowned, with a lion's mouth and bear paws, snarling and shouting.

Make a mosaic pen holder

You will need:
polystyrene cup • PVA glue • glue brush • macaroni pasta shapes (dry) • paints and paintbrush

What you do:

1 Starting at the base of the polystyrene cup, glue on the macaroni shapes one at a time. Build up the pattern in threes to make square tiles. Place the tiles in different directions.

2 When you have finished sticking on the macaroni shapes and they have dried, paint them in bright colours. Think of each set of three macaroni shapes as a mosaic tile, and paint them in different colours.

3 Leave your pen holder to dry.

4 When it is dry, place your pens in it and let it take pride of place on your desk!

Make a patterned place mat

You will need:
coloured sugar paper • A4 piece of card • squared paper • safety scissors • coloured pens or pencils • ruler • glue stick • laminator and laminating sheets or sticky-backed plastic sheets

What you do:

1 Draw out a rough design for your place mat on squared paper. Why not try a **symmetrical** pattern?

2 Cut the coloured sugar paper into strips about 1cm wide, and then cut the strips so that you have lots of little tiles. You may want to use a pencil and ruler to mark out the measurements.

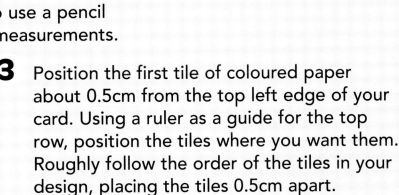

3 Position the first tile of coloured paper about 0.5cm from the top left edge of your card. Using a ruler as a guide for the top row, position the tiles where you want them. Roughly follow the order of the tiles in your design, placing the tiles 0.5cm apart.

4 Stick the tiles down onto the card with a glue stick as you go.

5 When you've finished making your pattern, you may want to protect it by **laminating** it or covering it in sticky-backed plastic.

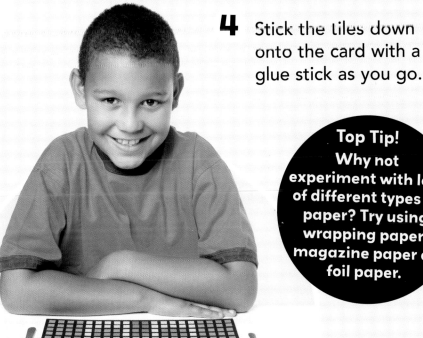

Top Tip! Why not experiment with lots of different types of paper? Try using wrapping paper, magazine paper or foil paper.

Make a mosaic photo frame

What you do:

1 Decide what shape you want your frame to be: square, circular or maybe something more unusual. Sketch it out on the cereal box card. Don't forget to include the hole for the photo!

2 Cut out your frame using scissors. You may need an adult to help you to cut the central hole.

Top Tip!
You can try using lots of different materials to decorate your frame. What about glass beads, pebbles, bottle tops or shells?

3 Arrange the collection of buttons around the frame until you're happy with the result. It doesn't matter if some stick out over the edge – in fact, it adds to the effect! Be careful not to cover the central hole.

4 Stick the buttons on with PVA glue.

5 Turn your frame on to its front and apply some glue around the edges of the photo hole. Lay your photo face down over the hole and press it down firmly.

6 Stick some ribbon or string on to the back of your frame using strong tape.

7 Hang up your frame.

Make a wall border

What you do:

1 Cut out a piece of wall lining paper using safety scissors. It could be A4 or A3, depending on the wall space available.

2 Sketch out the design you want to feature on the wall lining paper. Why not do this activity with friends or classmates and create a scene from Noah's Ark, like that on page 16?

like that on page 16?

You will need: wall lining paper • different coloured paper • safety scissors • glue stick • pencil • sticky-backed plastic

3 Cut or tear squares of different coloured paper and keep each colour in a separate pile.

4 Position and glue the tiles on to your sketch. You may have to cut some of the pieces to fit.

5 Cover your completed picture with sticky-backed plastic to protect it.

6 Put all the different pictures together to create a long wall border.

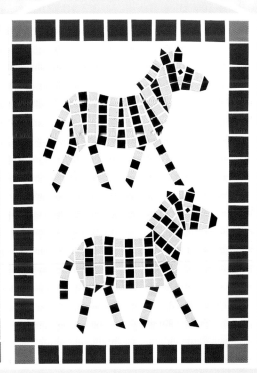

Glossary

abstract   in art, this describes works (pictures, sculptures, etc.) that consist of colours and shapes, without any recognisable figures or objects

adhesive   any substance that sticks one thing to another

Battle of Britain   war in the air, waged in the summer of 1940 between the attacking Germans and Britain's Royal Air Force (RAF)

Blitz (the)   the nickname given to the very heavy bombing of British cities during the Second World War

caduceus   the staff carried by the Greek god Hermes (called Mercury by the Romans)

cartoon   full-scale drawing, made as part of an artist's preparation for a mosaic, painting or other work

composition   the way a picture is arranged to make it pleasing or striking

direct method   the simplest method of creating a mosaic, by drawing a design on a surface and putting tesserae directly on to it

grout   an adhesive mixture of sand and cement, inserted between tiles or tesserae

indirect method   see reverse method

insignia   badges or symbols

laminating   covering and bonding with a thin, transparent sheet of plastic

Middle Ages   the period of European history between about 500 and 1500 CE

myths   stories about the long-distant past, usually including legends about the creation of the world and human beings. Myths often feature gods, heroes and monsters

Old Testament   the oldest part of the Bible. It describes the history and religion of the Jewish people in ancient times

reverse method   method of creating a mosaic, using a mirror-image drawing or cartoon

studio   the place where an artist works

symmetrical   describes a design or object that is exactly balanced, so that, for example, both halves are the same shape and colour

tesserae   small, fairly regular pieces of stone, glass or ceramic, used to make a mosaic. The singular (just one piece) is tessera

tube station   a station on London's Underground railways

Find out more

Books to read

Amazing Mosaics by Sarah Kelly (Red Fox Press, 2000)
Fun with Mosaic by Evelyn Bennett (Salamander, 1996)
Mosaics by Michelle Powell (Search Press, 2001)

These are more advanced, but very well illustrated, with inspiring ideas:
Classic Mosaic by Elaine M. Goodwin (Apple, 2000)
Design Sourcebook: Mosaics by Martin Cheek (New Holland, 2003)
The Complete Pebble Mosaic Handbook by Maggy Howarth (Firefly, 2003)

Websites to visit

Visit The Joy of Shards (www.thejoyofshards.co.uk). It is a superb general site that's full of interesting examples, advice and ideas.

The website Design a Mosaic (www.gwydir.demon.co.uk/jo/mosaic/index.htm) is very friendly and enthusiastic. It includes 'Make a Roman mosaic online' and other fun features.

Community Mosaic (www.savetheworldclub.org/mosaic.htm) shows the excellent results that can be achieved when everybody in a school is involved in making a mosaic.

Another fine communal project is on view at Cywaith Cymru (Artworks Wales) Caernarvon Mosaics (www.cywaithcymru.org/eng/commissions_detail.php?projectsID=180).

Places to go

London has lots of places to see mosaics. The British Museum, London, has the most varied collection of mosaics, incuding examples from Roman Britain, the Middle Ages, the Islamic world and Aztec Mexico. Boris Anrep's mosaics (p18/19) are on the floor around the main entrance of The National Gallery. The Hitchcock mosaics (p12/13) can be seen at Leytonstone Underground station in east London. If you visit the Houses of Parliament in Westminster, you could stop for a moment and look at the 19th century mosaics of saints in the Central Lobby. Nearby Westminster Cathedral has been decorated with mosaics since the early 20th century, so it contains modern religious works in a number of styles. The walls of Tottenham Court Road Underground station are covered with a series of colourful modernistic mosaics by the famous Scottish artist Sir Eduardo Paolozzi.

Two sites in West Sussex are furnished with fine Roman-British mosaics: Fishbourne Roman Palace, near Chichester, and Bignor Roman Villa.

There are outstanding collections of Roman mosaics at Corinium Museum, Cirencester, Gloucester; Dorset County Museum, Dorchester; and East Riding and Hull Museum, Hull, Yorkshire.

Rose Street in the centre of Edinburgh is popular with tourists. There are floor pebble mosaics by Maggy Howarth at the end of each section of the street.

Index

Photos or pictures are shown below in bold, **like this**.

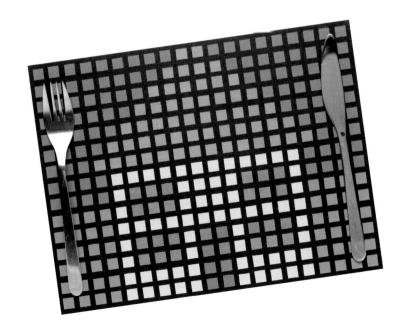